MORE
STREET
JEWELLERY
C Baglee & A Morley
NC
New Cavendish Books

Companion volume –
STREET JEWELLERY
A History of Enamel Advertising Signs
Christopher Baglee & Andrew Morley
ISBN 0 904568 21 0

More Street Jewellery first edition
published in Great Britain
by New Cavendish Books, 1982.

Designed by Badge Group Design, Newcastle upon Tyne
in association with John Cooper

Cover Enamel Sign, Garnier Signs
Original – size: 30″×24″. Date: c.1910
Collection: Baglee/Morley
Colour separations, Aragorn
Printed and bound in Holland
Setting and mono illustration, Western Printing Services Ltd

New Cavendish Books
11 New Fetter Lane, London EC4P 4EE
Marketing: North Way, Andover, Hants. SP10 5BE

ISBN 0 904568 39 3

Size: 24"×32". Date: c.1908. Maker: Chromographic Enamel Co Collection: Baglee/Morley

Contents

HUDSON'S SOAP
J. ADAMSON
FAMILY GROCER
CADBURY'S
CHOCOLATE
FRY'S
300 PRIZE MEDALS
CHOCOLATE
VAN HOUTEN'S COCOA
NESTLE'S MILK

Preface

Since the publication of *Street Jewellery* and the touring exhibition of our collection '100 Years of Enamel Signs', in 1978, we have met many other avid collectors and enthusiasts, who have allowed us access to their hidden hoards of enamels, many of which were previously unknown to us, and never before published.

The response to *Street Jewellery*, which was the first book on its subject, proved that enamel advertising signs, which up to that time had been the preserve of a few dedicated dealers, collectors and photographers, had a wide, general appeal. This reached out to the general collectors of advertising ephemera (who could augment their specialisation, such as bottles, with a few well chosen signs), to the amateur social historian, who could find fresh evidence of the social forms and functions of this kind of street advertising, and to the vast majority of the general public over the age of twenty, for whom the medium was a living memory, and in whom pleasantly nostalgic reveries were aroused by seeing these once familiar images again. Stimulation of interest in the subject has also been seen in the number of products produced by commercial enterprises directly inspired by *Street Jewellery*, and including wallpaper, wrapping papers, reproduction signs and miniature model railway posters, all based on our book and collection.

As a result of this wide interest in enamel signs, we have somehow become the natural 'sorting office' of information and contact between collectors, who have constantly asked us for a follow-up to *Street Jewellery*. This fraternity of enamel sign collectors has grown into a nationwide network of enamelophiles, without whose commitment we would not have been able to produce this new book, illustrating as it does the cream of pictorial enamel signs from over thirty different collections. This volume is intended to compliment *Street Jewellery*, as well as being a showcase in its own right for some of the best pictorial enamels not previously included in *Street Jewellery*, or elsewhere. We have tried to resist the temptation of repeating old favourites, but occasionally we have found it desirable to reproduce some again in order to make direct visual comparisons with new discoveries, or else to present them in a larger format. With very few exceptions, therefore, the pictorial signs illustrated here have never been seen in print before and we believe that very few examples of good pictorial enamels known to ourselves and our fellow collectors have been overlooked.

Street Jewellery still stands as the authoritative history of enamelled iron advertising signs, as well as giving the most thoroughly comprehensive cross-section of representative types. However, we hope that with the publication of *More Street Jewellery*, we have revealed the great richness of quality existing in the very best examples of pictorial enamel signs. We also hope that this work will encourage its readers to discover and preserve still further items of fine street jewellery, and that even more exciting examples will come to light, and feed the ever growing enthusiasm for this subject.

C.B. & A.M.
Newcastle upon Tyne, 1981

Size: 39"×21"
Date: c.1890
Maker: Patent Enamel Co
Collection: Paul Davies

Acknowledgements

The preparation of this book would have been impossible without the generous co-operation of many friends and associates. It is difficult to allot credit fairly for so much kind help, taking as it did so many forms. However, we feel that primarily we must give special thanks to those collectors of enamel advertising signs who kindly allowed us to photograph their signs for reproduction in this volume. We must also give special mention – for their practical help – to Ken King and Mike Standen, who both travelled many miles, and spent many hours, seeking out and photographing signs which were otherwise inaccessible to us. Also included in the following credit list are some of the many people and organisations whose help in providing material, information and advice has proved invaluable to us in our task.

Badge Group Design, Bass Museum, Beamish North of England Open Air Museum County Durham, Jeremy Biggs, Peter Birch, Alan Blakeman, Bluebell Railway, Bourton-on-the-Water Motor Museum, G. Braekman, Society for Environmental Cultural Care (Vereniging vor Kulturele Milieuzorg VZW, Gent), David C. C. Brown, J. W. Brown, Bob Buxton, Nat Chait, L.P.C., Colman's Foods, Paul Davies, Mary Dixon, Dodo Old Advertising, Eddie Dunks, Graham Eastwood, Liz Farrow, Mick and Jackie Forbes, Jim Gilroy, Christopher Gordon, Erica Gorman, David Griffith and Josephine Wright, John Hawkins, Heinz, R. J. Hill, Alan Hooper, Ironbridge Gorge Museum, Ed Jaques, K. B. King, Allen Levy, Stafford Linsley, Leslie Longstaff, Bill McAlpine, N. Van Maldegen, K. A. Maskall, Somerset Moore, Roy Morgan, Bob Mouland, Dave Nelson, The Old Fashioned Cobbler, Robert Opie, Barrie Pook, Valerie Pragnall, Howard Raine, Relic Designs, Tom Richards, Stewart Rickards, Spencer Rutter, Mike Standen, The Star Cafe, David Stevens, Neville Summers, Frank Thornton, Vaux Breweries, Alan Wall, Walter Willson.

Thanks must also go to those collectors and enthusiasts of enamel signs and other old advertising, who, since the publication of *Street Jewellery* and the exhibition tour of our collection, have contacted us with information and encouragement, and to all our friends and relations, in particular Mavis Baglee, for their continued support.

Photo Credits

All photographs by Andrew Morley except those by:

Christopher Baglee
Gaston Braekman
Mike Cavanagh
L.P.C.
Paul Davies
Geoffrey Goddard
David E. Griffiths
John Hawkins
R. J. Hill
Mick Jones
K. B. King
Maurice Lovett
Geoff Marston
Robert Opie
Pentalow
Philipson Studios
George Pope
Valerie Pragnell
Relic Designs
Peter Simpkin
Mike Standen
David Stevens
Maurice Turner
Peter Williams
Yorkshire Post

Size: 18"×48". Date: 1920s. Collection: Mick Forbes

Size: 21"×23". Date: 1930s. Collection: Bourton Motor Museum

COCOA
COLMAN'S
MUSTARD
VIM
RUBICON
BARRINGTON STREET
Brooke
Bond
Tea
COLMAN'S
WASH BLUE
FRYS
COCOA
WOODBINES
STAR
LYONS
CRAVEN A
DIGGER
CRAVEN
DIGGER

CROSS
MILK
KENSITAS
KENSITAS
KOMO
DYMO
MILK
CROSS
MILK

Introduction

The design concept for enamel advertising signs, having originated in the mid-Victorian era, largely retained the visual qualities of the early days throughout a century of major production. More than a score of sign manufacturers, some with their own designers, put out hundreds, even thousands, of individual designs, reproduced each time in hundreds or thousands in the permanent medium of glass fused to steel. Although most of the artists responsible for the creation of these designs have remained anonymous, their styles can sometimes be recognised in different signs, and attribution can be reinforced by the occasional inclusion of the manufacturer's name on the bottom corner of a sign, leading one to the recognition of a 'house style'. The products of Chromo of Wolverhampton, and Patent Enamel of Birmingham are especially easy to identify.

The many companies involved – all now defunct – included not only those mentioned above, but also The Imperial Enamel Company of Birmingham, The Falkirk Iron Company and Jordon's of Bilston; all these companies' work exhibiting the highest artistic standards. Few documents record the output of enamel sign manufacturers, but the two catalogues, parts of which were illustrated in *Street Jewellery* and the catalogue of Jordan's of Bilston, demonstrate the pride that each firm took in showing off its quality of design. An interesting adjunct to these sample catalogues is a trade sample sign, produced by the Patent Enamel Company *c.*1910 (p. 17). This sign – quite charming as an artifact in itself – is not truly a pictorial design, and yet clearly illustrates the qualities and potential of the produce being advertised, namely the sign itself and some of the range of colours available for use. Actually these particular colours are not really representative of those generally used in Patent's signs. More often the primary shades of blue, red and yellow, reinforced by stark black and white, were employed. Less frequently used were brown, green, orange, maroon and light blue. Only the most expensive and elaborate signs were made in the more exotic pastel and pale earth colours, illustrated in this sample.

Readers of our first book, *Street Jewellery*, will have received a comprehensive introduction to the typical design methods of this medium, including both signs which were very simply designed, containing only lettering and few colours at one end of the scale, and at the other end, designs conceived as complete images, incorporating both pictorial elements and lettering in full colour. The latter category is by the general assent of collectors and enthusiasts the most interesting manifestation of the designer's art in enamel, and it is for this reason that, since the publication of *Street Jewellery*, our attention has been concentrated on pictorial signs, and in this book we have excluded all but the most elegant purely lettered signs. The examples shown here give a fuller indication of the types and styles, techniques and range of pictorial enamels, than was previously possible.

Although most of the designers have, as stated, remained anonymous – probably because of their low status as employees of an advertiser or sign manufacturer, a few celebrated names have remained linked to certain signs. The popularity of the new wave of English designers at the turn of the century in book illustration, newspaper advertising, theatre and travel posters, etc., made them attractive as designers to the enamel advertising sign trade.

Size: 18"×18". Date: c.1910. Collection: Stafford Linsley

Aubrey Beardsley was the progenitor of this new style, but alas, as far as we know, there are no enamels by his hand extant. However enamels survive from several of his followers and imitators, including some by the Beggarstaffs (the pseudonym of Sir William Nicholson and James Pryde), John Hassall, Tom Browne, Septimus E. Scott and (better known as a horse painter than a designer) Sir Alfred Munnings. The essence of their style, now known as 'poster style' normally consists of opposing tones captured in a sinuous line. The flavour is reminiscent of the crude chap book woodcut blended with the more refined Japanese woodcut, and laced together by Art Nouveau. A combination of the visual results of these relief print techniques (as distinct from their means of production), when applied to the design of an enamel sign, was particularly appropriate, as the stencilling method of producing an enamel sign is essentially very similar in its visual qualities. Examples of pure black and white tonality are the *c.*1905 P. & R. Hay crinolined ladies by J. W. Simpson, the 'Three Generations' design for Rowntree's Elect Cocoa of 1899, (originally a poster by the Beggarstaffs) and the anonymous continental RVS insurance sign. Of similar technique and style, but incorporating areas of plain colour in black lines, are Hassall's Morse's Distemper series and Bibby's Cream Equivalent (p. 35) usually attributed to Tom Browne. Tom Browne certainly produced interesting lithographic images for Fry's chocolate (p. 33) which, having a full tonal range (originally designed for paper posters) are still redolent of the late Victorian, early Edwardian taste, for picturesque simplification. The power of this 'So near . . .' sign as a black and white image is highlighted when it is contrasted with the aesthetically unsuccessful attempt to produce a colour washed version. Far more successful as a colour design is the delightfully bold and humourous concept of a publican devised for Bullards Beers by Munnings (p. 67). A late example of the flat bold colour and black line style is the famous W. H. Smith 'Newsboy' designed by Septimus E. Scott in the late 1920s.

Without wishing to reiterate the factual information on manufacturing processes included in *Street Jewellery* we would like to add to it relevant additional notes about the other major means of producing images from enamel, apart from stencilling and lithography. Direct photographic transfers sometimes combined with tinting by hand were used, a representative and very beautiful example being the Player's Navy Cut Actress (p. 23), and without the tinting but with subtle retouching, the Jones' Sewing Machine 'Busy . . .' seamstress (p. 55). Early evidence of airbrushing is noticeable on the British Dominions sports car sign (p. 20), and on the Players' Navy Cut 'Hero's' lifebelt (p. 47). We have also discovered, on a particularly well preserved coloured Fry's 5 Boys, the use of direct brush applied enamel colour, to enhance lithographed print, and brushwork additions can be observed on the stencilled image of the 6′×4′ Palethorpes Sausage sign (p. 81), and again on the British Dominions sign.

Size: 36″×23″
Date: c.1899
Maker: Patent Enamel Co
Collection: Neville Summers

Size: 36"×18". Date: c.1930
Collection: Neville Summers

Size: 22"×12". Date: c.1899
Designer: J. W. Simpson.
Collection: Ed Jaques

Size: 21¼"×14". Date: 1899
Designer: Beggarstaff Brothers
Collection: Baglee/Morley

Size: 77"×37". Date: 1955
Maker: Foremail
Collection: G. Braekman

Size: 60"×35". Date: c.1925. Maker: Patent Enamel Co
Designer: John Hassall

Size: 22"×36". Date: 1905 1925
Maker: Chromographic Enamel Co Collection: Bluebell Railway

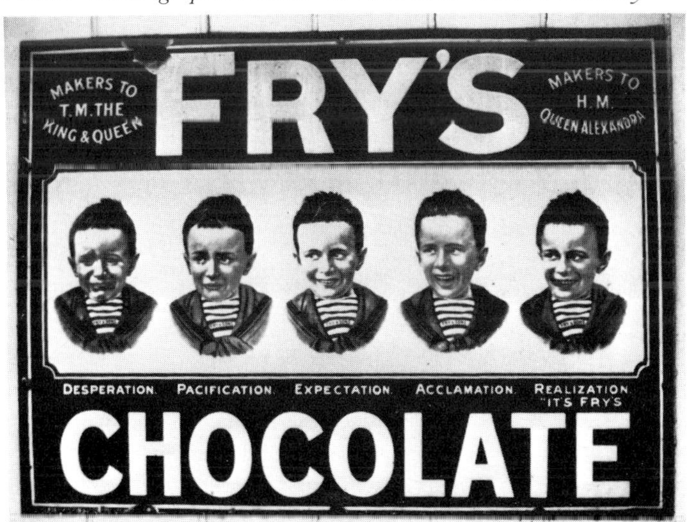

Size: 25"×16"
Date: 1920s
Designer: Septimus E. Scott
Collection: Baglee/Morley

F. COLLIER.
CLAY TOBACCO PIPE MANUFR
HORSE SHOERS
SCOTT & CROW.
FARRIERS & GENERAL SMITH
R. PRESTON.
WHOLESALE & RETAIL
BRUSH MANUFACTURER
KENYON
TITCOMB
"THE QUAY." HIGH ST GATESHEAD.
R. GIBSON.

Size: $6\frac{1}{2}$" diameter. Date: c.1900. Maker: Garnier & Co
Collection: Baglee/Morley

Size: 10"×21". Date: c.1900. Collection: David Griffith

Size: 20"×12"
Date: c.1900–1910
Collection: Mike Standen

Size: 12"×18". Date: 1930s. Collection: Baglee/Morley

Size: 14"×10"
Date: c.1905
Collection: David Stevens

Size: 24"×21"
Date: c.1950
Collection: Baglee/Morley

Illustrations from J. A. Jordan & Sons of Bilston, catalogue c.1928

Size: 9¾"×7". Date: c.1910. Maker: Patent Enamel Co Collection: David Griffith

Size approx 72"×30". Date: c.1890. Collection: The Old Fashioned Cobbler

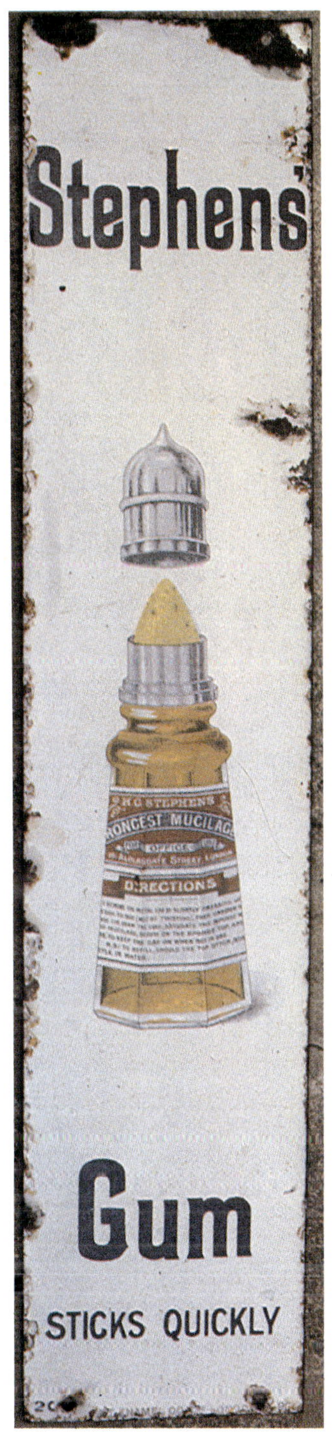

Size: 24"×5"
Date: c.1910
Maker: Patent Enamel Co
Collection: Robert Opie

Size: 12"×6"
Date: 1933
Collection: David Griffith

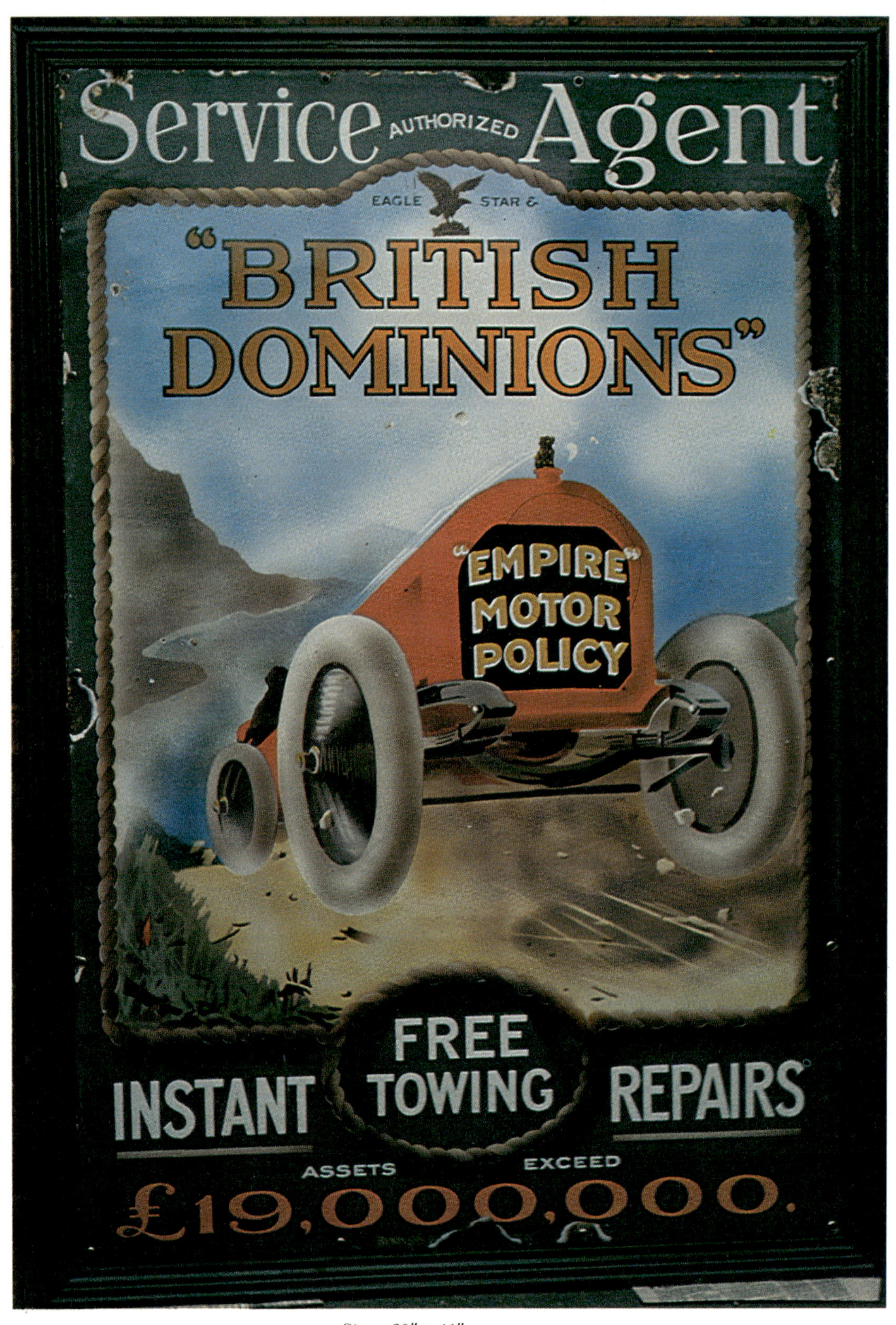

Size: 60"×41"
Date: c.1920
Maker: Business Builders, London
Collection: Baglee/Morley

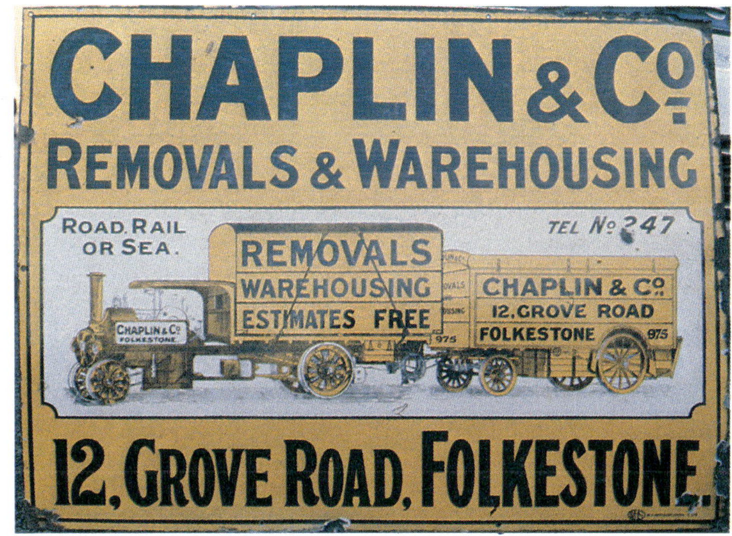

Size: 36"×48"
Date: c.1915
Maker: W.H.S.
Collection: John Hawkins

Size: 27"×36"
Date: c.1905
Collection: Tom Richards

Size: 36"×48". Date: c.1910. Collection: Bill McAlpine

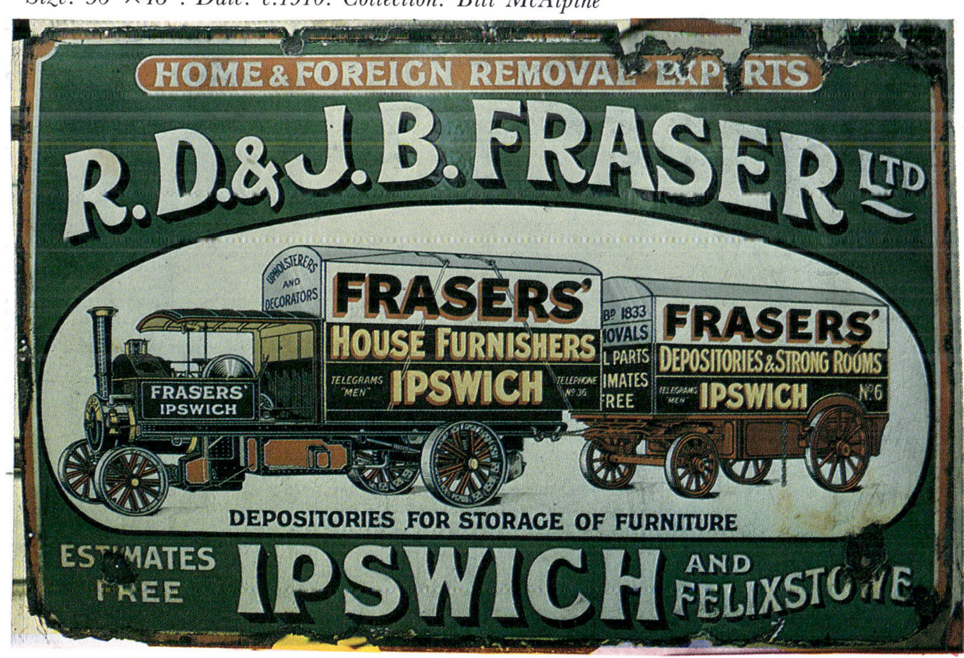

Size: 20"×15"
Date: c.1910
Maker: Imperial Enamel Co
Collection: Baglee/Morley

Size: diam $16\frac{3}{4}$"
Date: 1939
Collection: G. Braekman

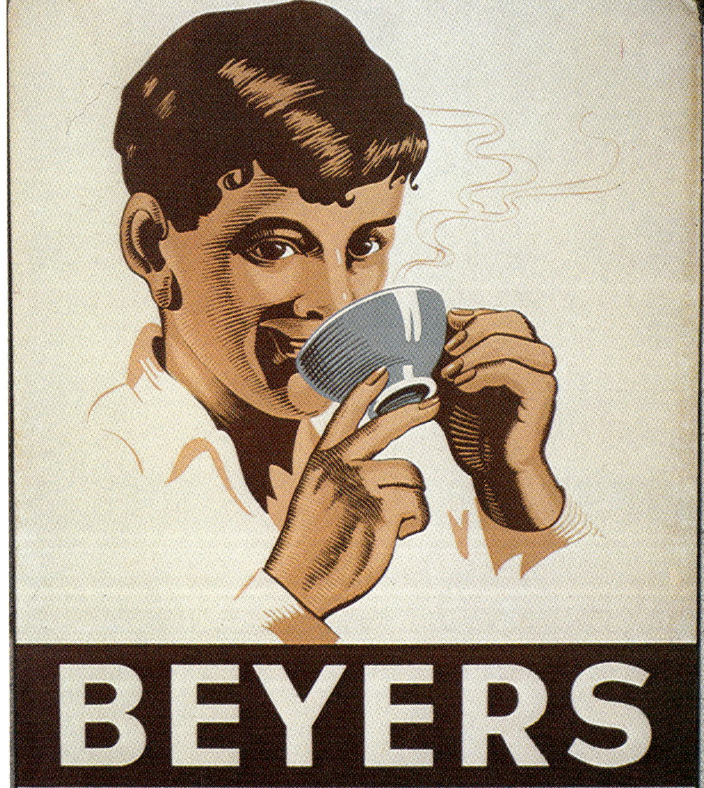

Size: 28"×20"
Date: 1954
Maker: Emaillerie Belge
Collection: G. Braekman

Size: 60"×30"
Date: c.1880
Collection: Somerset Moore

Size: 9″×6″
Date: c.1880
Collection: Bob Mouland

Size: 18″×46″
Date: c.1914
Maker: Chromographic Enamel Co
Collection: Allen Levy

Size: 38¾"×24"
Date: 1938
Maker: Emailleries de Koekelburg
Collection: G. Braekman

Size: 29"×19"
Date: c.1920
Maker: Imperial Enamel Co
Collection: Barrie Pook

Size: 23½"×15½"
Date: c.1935
Collection: David Griffith

Size: 36"×26¼"
Date: c.1905
Maker: Patent Enamel Co
Collection: Beamish Open Air Museum

Size: 22"×17"
Date: 1890s
Maker: Sir Joseph Causton
Collection: Mike Standen

Size: 18"×10"
Date: c.1905
Collection: David Griffith

Size: 10″×2¼″
Date: c.1910
Maker: Garnier & Co
Collection: Mike Standen

Size: 60″×40″
Date: c.1916
Maker: Griffiths & Browett
Collection: Eddie Dunks

Size: 20″×40″. Date: post-1915
Maker: Patent Enamel Co. Collection: Baglee/Morley

Size: 24"×36"
Date: c.1910
Maker: Chromographic Enamel Co
Collection: Bourton Motor Museum

Size: 36"×48"
Date: c.1905
Maker: Falkirk Iron Co
Collection: Baglee/Morley

Size: 23½"×11"
Date: c.1895
Maker: Patent Enamel Co
Collection: Spencer Rutter

Size: 10"×7"
Date: c.1910
Maker: Stainton & Hulme
Collection: Christopher Gordon

Size: 6"×15½"
Date: 1900
Maker: Falkirk Iron Co
Collection: Baglee/Morley

Size: 36"×24"
Date: c.1910
Collection: Dodo

Size: 40″×30″
Date: c.1910
Maker: Imperial Enamel Co
Collection: Spencer Rutter

Size: 30″×30″
Date: c.1900
Maker: Imperial Enamel Co
Collection: Christopher Gordon

Size: 39″×30″
Date: c.1890
Maker: Patent Enamel Co
Collection: Barrie Pook

Size: 24″×18″
Date: c.1930
Collection: Barrie Pook

Size: 9½″×3½″
Date: c.1890
Collection: David Griffith

Size: 16″×6″
Date: c.1890
Collection: David Griffith

Size: 20"×15"
Date: c.1935
Collection: Baglee/Morley

Size: 25"×16"
Date: c.1925
Collection: Dodo

Size: 12"×18"
Date: c.1930
Collection: Baglee/Morley

Size: 14"×10"
Date: c.1907
Collection: Barrie Pook

Size: 14"×10"
Date: c.1907
Collection: Neville Summers

Size: 10"×14"
Date: c.1907
Collection: Neville Summers

Size: 60"×40"
Date: c.1925
Designer: John Hassall
Collection: David Brown

Size: 60"×40"
Date: c.1925
Designer: John Hassall
Collection: Baglee/Morley

Size: 20"×33"
Date: c.1925
Maker: Patent Enamel Co
Collection: Star Cafe, Soho

Size: 36″×26¼″
Date: c.1902
Maker: Patent Enamel Co
Designer: Tom Browne
Collection: Beamish Open Air Museum

Size: 12"×60". Date: c.1935
Collection: Baglee/Morley

Size: 18"×60". Date: c.1935
Collection: Graham Eastwood

Size: 18"×60". Date: c.1935
Collection: Graham Eastwood

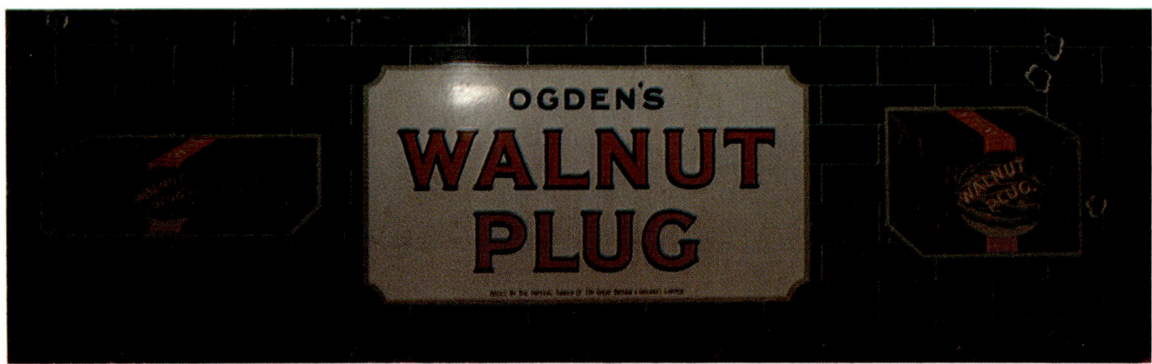

Size: 18"×60". Date: c.1935
Collection: Graham Eastwood

Size: 30"×22"
Date: c.1890
Collection: David Griffith

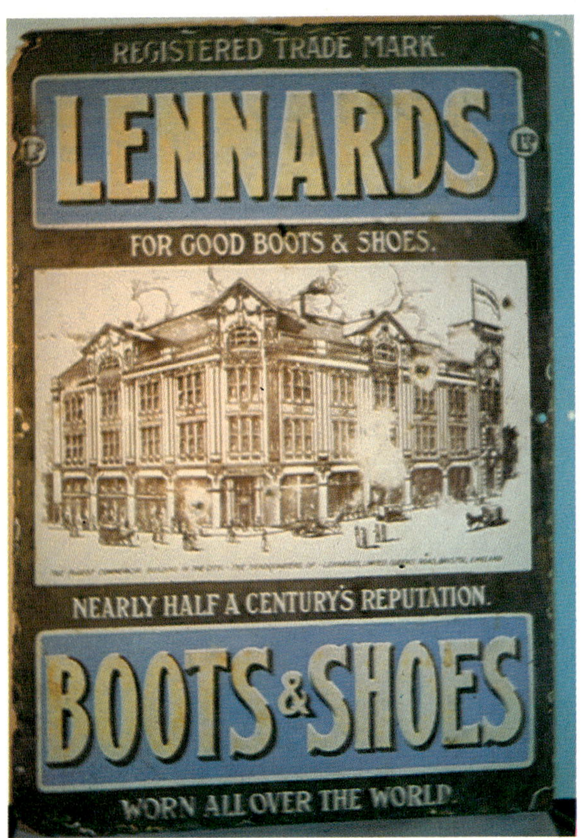

Size: $19\frac{1}{2}'' \times 13\frac{1}{2}''$
Date: c.1910
Collection: Bourton Motor Museum

Size: $9'' \times 13''$
Date: c.1900
Collection: Barrie Pook

Size: 29"×19"
Date: c.1938
Collection: Baglee/Morley

Size: 36"×24"
Date: c.1905
Maker: Patent Enamel Co
Collection: Spencer Rutter

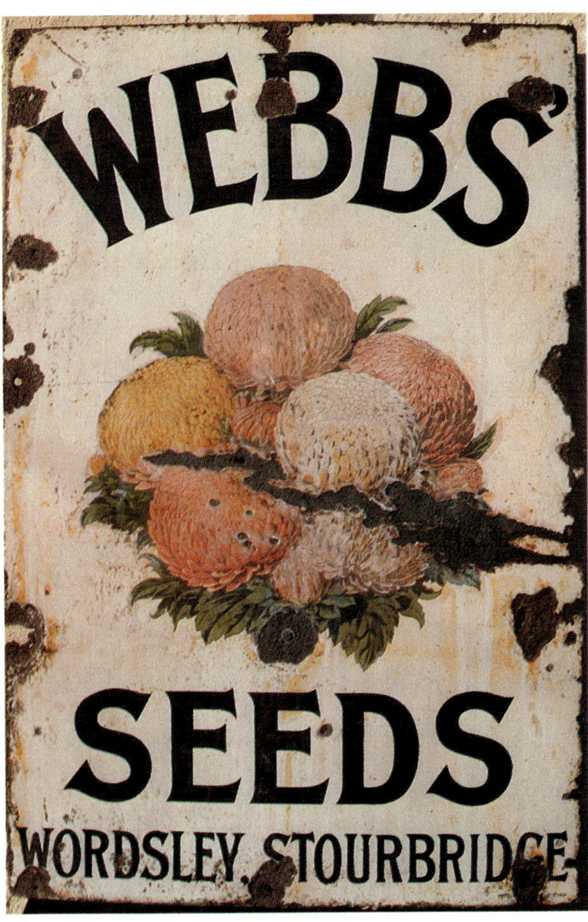

Size: 9"×12"
Date: c.1911
Maker: Chromographic Enamel Co
Collection: Somerset Moore

Size: 33" diameter
Collection: Heinz

Size: 18"×11½"
Date: c.1910
Maker: Falkirk Iron Co
Collection: Dodo

Size: 35"×24"
Date: 1935
Collection: G. Braekman

Size: 59"×37"
Date: 1950
Maker: Emailleries de Koekelberg
Collection: G. Braekman

ize: 8"×12"
ate: 1955
esigner: Car Veelenturf
ollection: Baglee/Morley

Size: 12″×16″
Date: 1920s
Collection: Mike Standen

Size: 17″×11″
Date: 1890s
Maker: Imperial Enamel Co
Collection: Neville Summers

Size: 15½″ diameter
Date: 1950s
Maker: Austria Email
Collection: L.P.C.

Size: 20″×30″
Date: c.1900
Collection: Dodo

Size: $5\frac{1}{2}$″×25″
Date: 1920s
Collection: Baglee/Morley

Size: $5\frac{1}{2}$″×25″
Date: 1920s
Collection: Baglee/Morley

Size: 30"×20"
Date: 1912
Collection: Dodo

Size: 54"×18"
Date: 1950s
Maker: Emaillerie Belge
Collection: Baglee/Morley

Size: 36"×24"
Collection: Somerset Moore

Size: 16"×12"
Maker: Patent Enamel Co
Collection: Neville Summers

Date: 1896
Collection: Bluebell Railway

Size: 43½"×31½"
Date: 1926
Maker: Emailleries Koekelberg
Collection: G. Braekman

Size: 40"×26"
Date: 1911
Maker: Patent Enamel Co
Collection: Baglee/Morley

Size: 10"×12"
Date: c.1916
Maker: Burnham's
Collection: John Hawkins

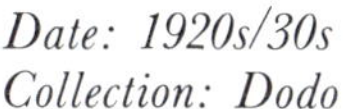

Date: 1920s/30s
Collection: Dodo

Size: 30"×20"
Date: 1920s/40s
Collection: Baglee/Morley

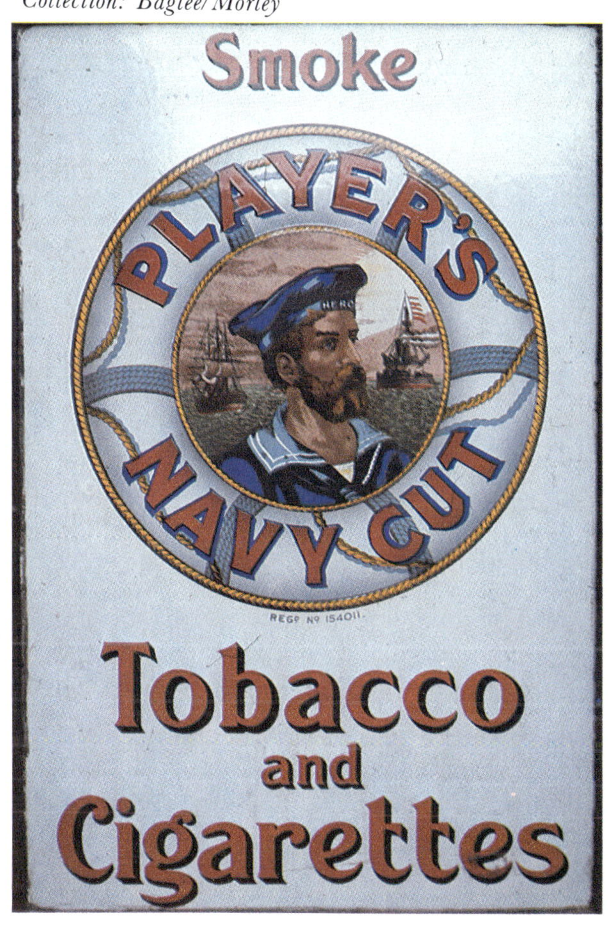

Size: 20"×15"
Date: 1920s/30s
Collection: Christopher Gordon

Size: 30"×22"
Date: 1920s/40s
Collection: Christopher Gordon

Size: 42″×27″
Date: 1930s
Collection: Barrie Pook

Size: 26" diameter
Date: 1930s
Collection: NEPWAC

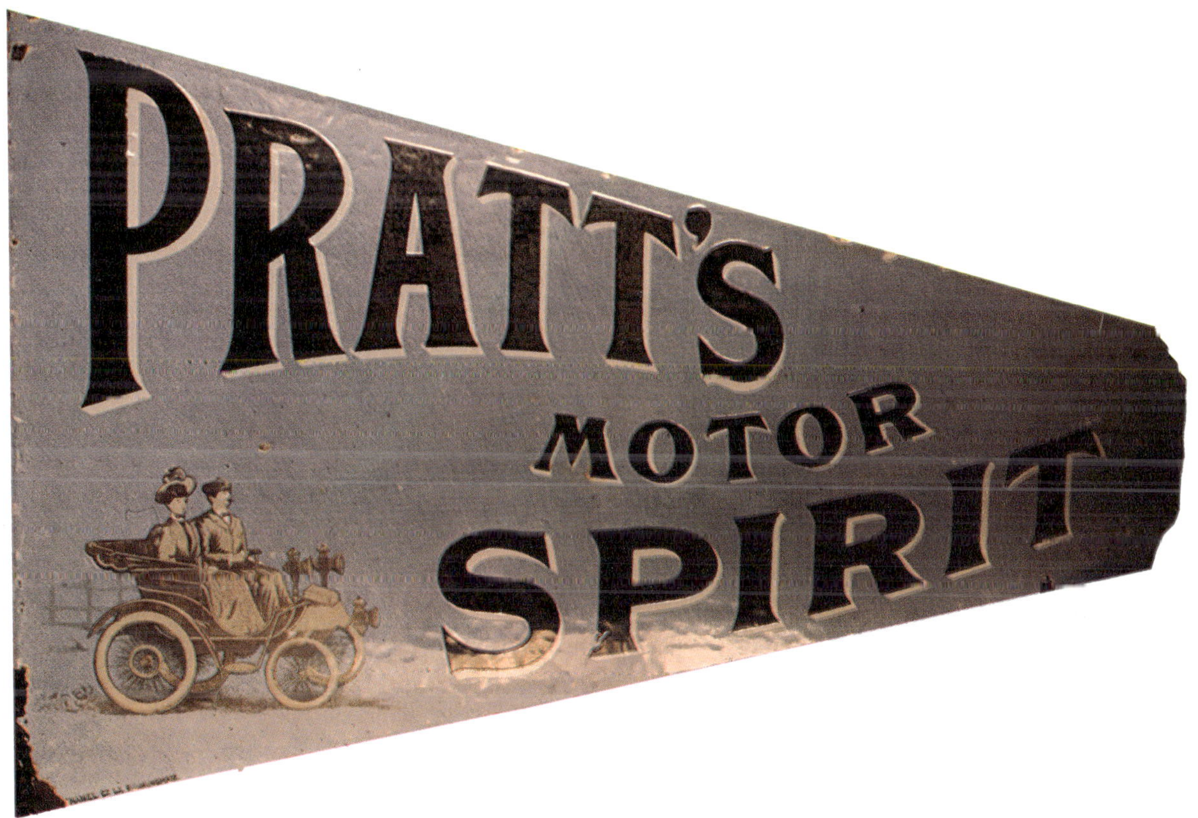

Size: 15"×22"
Date: c.1910
Collection: Bourton Motor Museum

Size: 28″×20″
Date: 1920s
Collection: Barrie Pook

Size: 28″×20″
Date: c.1919
Collection: Peter Birch

SHELL lubricating OILS
SHELL
FROM THE PUMP
SHELL
MOTOR OIL
SHELL-MEX LTD
KINGSWAY, LONDON W.C.2
SHELL

Size: 36″×9″
Date: 1920s
Maker: Jordan's
Collection: Bill McAlpine

Size: 24″×8″
Date: 1900
Maker: Chromographic Enamel Co
Collection: Baglee/Morley

Size: 14″×9″
Date: c.1930
Collection: Somerset Moore

Size: 30″×20″
Collection: Peter Birch

Size: $24\frac{1}{2}''\times 37''$
Date: 1920s
Collection: Baglee/Morley

Size: $28''\times 18''$
Date: 1920s
Maker: Hölzl, Vienna
Collection: L.P.C.

Size: $23''\times 15''$
Date: 1930s
Maker: Ferro Email
Collection: L.P.C.

Size: 11″×7½″
Date: 1910
Collection: David Griffith

Size: 32½″×34½″
Date: 1900
Maker: Patent Enamel Co
Collection: Baglee/Morley

Size: 36″×27″
Date: 1930s
Maker: Willings & Co
Collection: Barrie Pook

Size: 37″×24½″
Date: 1920s
Collection: Baglee/Morley

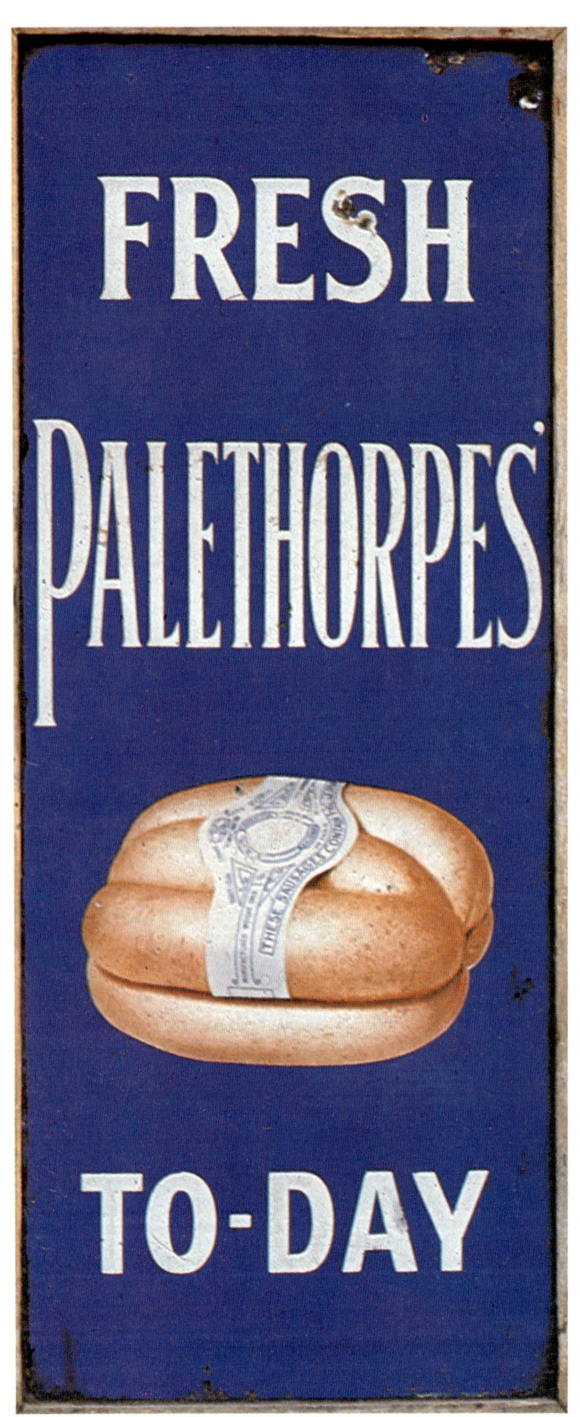

Size: 36" × 15"
Date: 1920s
Maker: Bruton
Collection: Baglee/Morley

Size: 36" × 15"
Date: 1920s
Maker: Bruton
Collection: Baglee/Morley

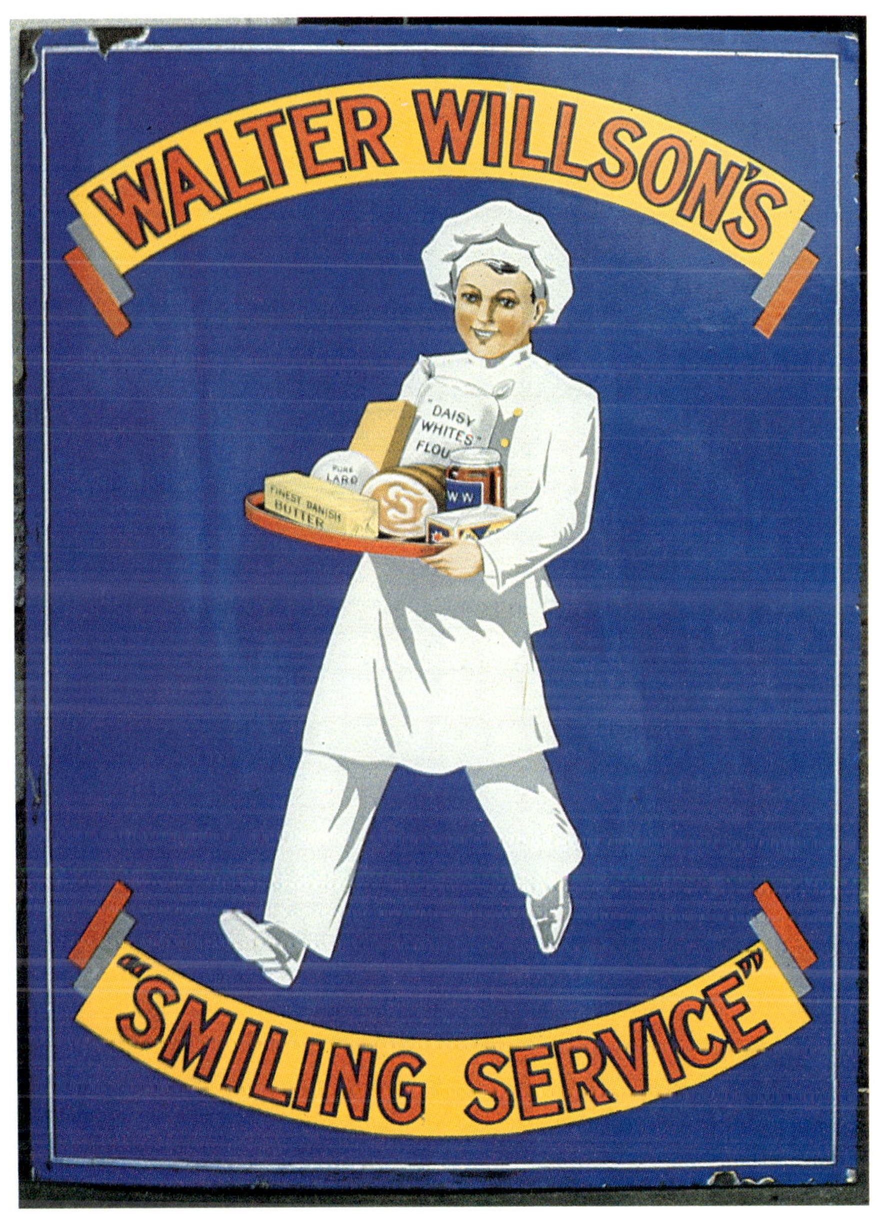

Size: 27"×20"
Date: 1920s
Collection: Walter Willson

Size: 42"×32"
Date: 1890
Collection: Dodo

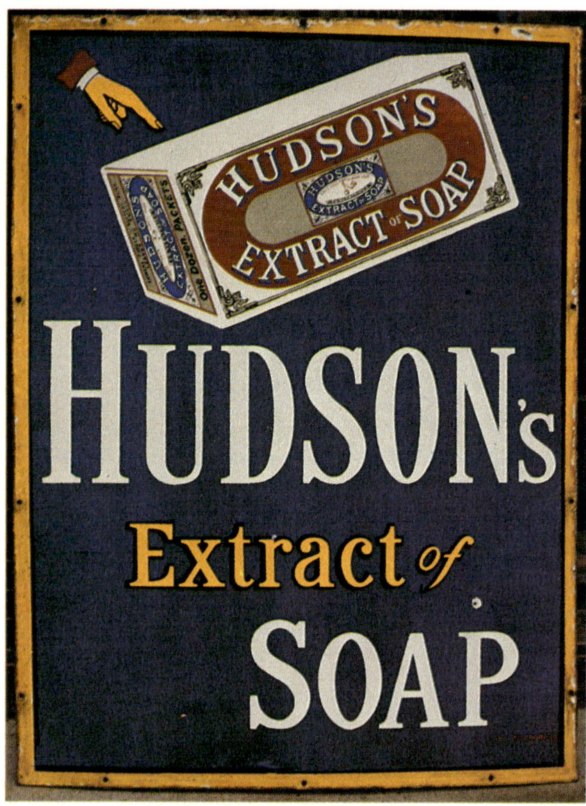

Size: 30"×20"
Date: c.1935
Collection: Baglee/Morley

Size: 36"×24"
Date: 1920
Collection: Erica Gorman

Size: 6"×15¾"
Date: 1930s
Collection: Dodo

Size: 13"×19" Date: c.1905
Maker: Patent Enamel Co
Collection: Barrie Pook

Size: 60"×36"
Date: 1885
Collection: Jeremy Biggs

Size: 22"×5"
Date: 1905
Collection: David Griffith

Size: 26¾"×18¾"
Date: 1936
Maker: Emailleries Koekelberg
Collection: G. Braekman

Size: 30"×24"
Date: 1915
Maker: Imperial Enamel Co
Collection: Dodo

Size: 12"×18"
Date: 1900
Maker: Trenner & Son London
Collection: Christopher Gordon

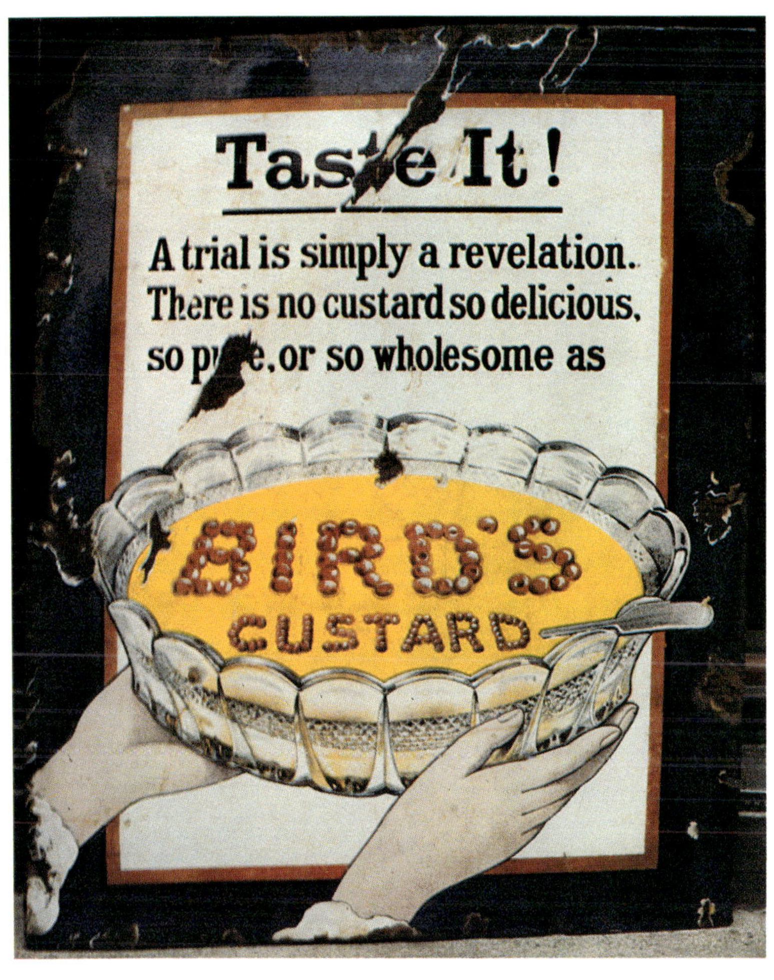

Size: 30"×24"
Date: 1915
Maker: Imperial Enamel Co
Collection: Christopher Gordon

Size: 36"×24"
Date: 1900
Collection: Dodo

Size: 17"×11½"
Date: 1910
Collection: David Griffith

Size: 12"×12"
Date: c.1918
Maker: Patent Enamel Co
Collection: Mick Forbes

Date: 1900s. Maker: Falkirk Iron Co
Collection: Baglee/Morley

Date: c.1915. Maker: Falkirk Iron Co
Collection: Baglee/Morley

Date: c.1920. Maker: 'Hanker' Mitcham
Collection: Baglee/Morley.

Date: c.1900. Maker: Universal, Bilston
Collection: Beamish Open Air Museum

Size: 18″×7½″
Date: c.1898
Collection: Baglee/Morley

Size: 18″×6½″
Date: c.1896
Maker: Chromographic Enamel Co
Collection: John Hawkins

Size: 20″×30″
Date: 1925
Collection: Valerie Pragnall

Size: 40″×60″
Date: 1910
Collection: Bass Museum

Size: 18"×10"
Date: 1920
Designer: Sir A. Munnings
Collection: Barrie Pook

Size: 30"×20"
Date: 1910
Maker: Stocal
Collection: Barrie Pook

Size: 37"×29"
Date: 1936
Maker: Emaillerie Belge
Collection: G. Brackman

Size: 30"×24"
Date: 1890
Collection: Baglee/Morley

Size: 30"×20"
Date: c.1925
Collection: David Griffith

Size: 18″×10½″
Date: c.1900
Collection: Baglee/Morley

Size: 18″×10½″
Date: c.1900
Collection: Christopher Gordon

Size: 24″×24″
Date: c.1900
Collection: Bluebell Railway

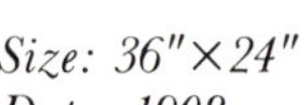

Size: 36″×24″
Date: 1908
Maker: Chromographic Enamel Co
Collection: Baglee/Morley

Size: 18"×12"
Date: 1910
Collection: Somerset Moore

Size: 18"×36"
Date: 1911
Maker: Chromographic Enamel Co
Collection: Baglee/Morley

Size: 36"21"
Date: 1880
Collection: David Griffith

Size: 66"×40"
Date: 1905
Collection: Barrie Pook

Size: 19″×14½″
Date: post-1867
Maker: Willings & Co, London
Collection: Valerie Pragnall

Size: 13″×10″
Date: c.1910
Maker: J. A. Campbell, Belfast
Collection: Christopher Gordon

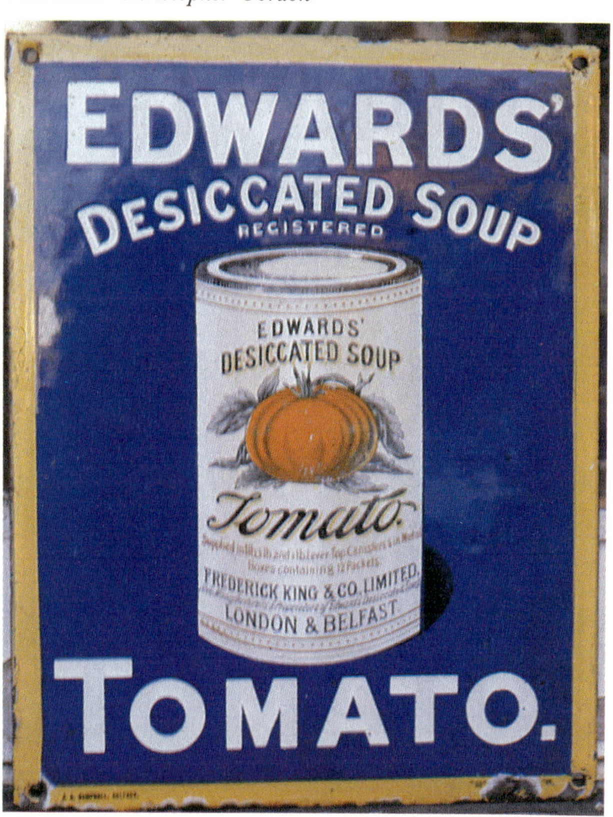

Size: 18″×12″
Date: c.1905
Collection: Baglee/Morley

Date: c.1910
Maker: Chromographic Enamel Co
Collection: Ironbridge Museum

Size: 40"×30"
Date: c.1920
Maker: Patent Enamel Co
Collection: Robert Opie

Size: 13"×10"
Date: 1920
Maker: G.B. & B.
Collection: Valerie Pragnall

Size: 72″×40″
Date: c.1905
Collection: Dodo

Size: 30″×20″
Date: 1925
Collection: Christopher Gordon

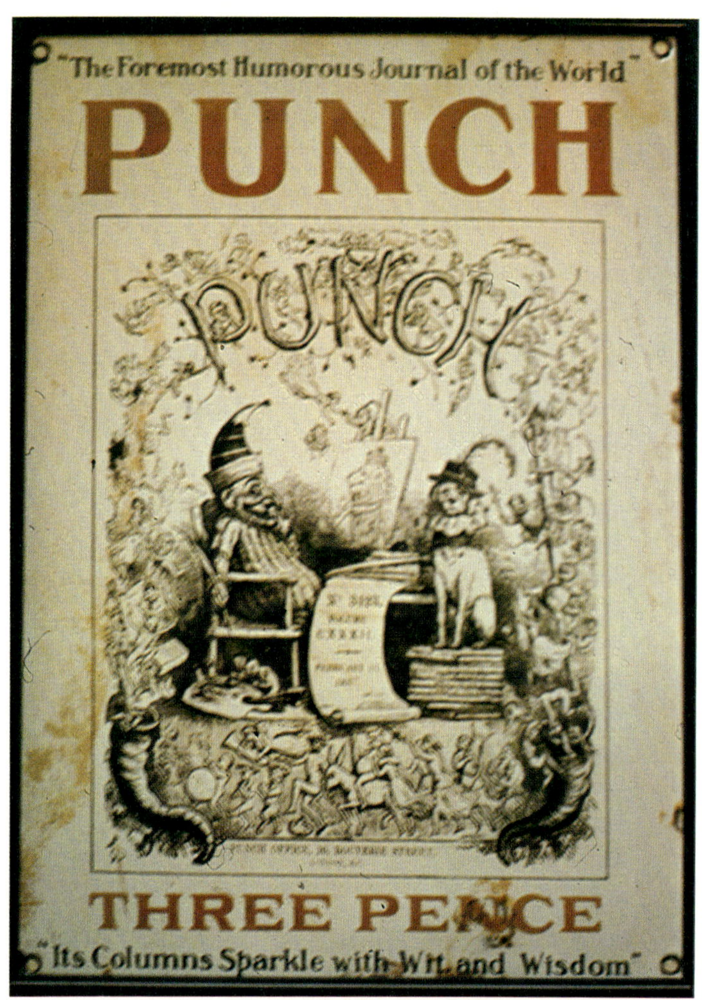

Size: 13½″×10″
Date: 1919
Collection: Peter Birch

Size: 18″×48″
Date: 1930
Collection: Dodo

Illustrations from J. A. Jordan & Son of Bilston, catalogue c.1928

Illustrations from J. A. Jordan & Son of Bilston, catalogue c.1928

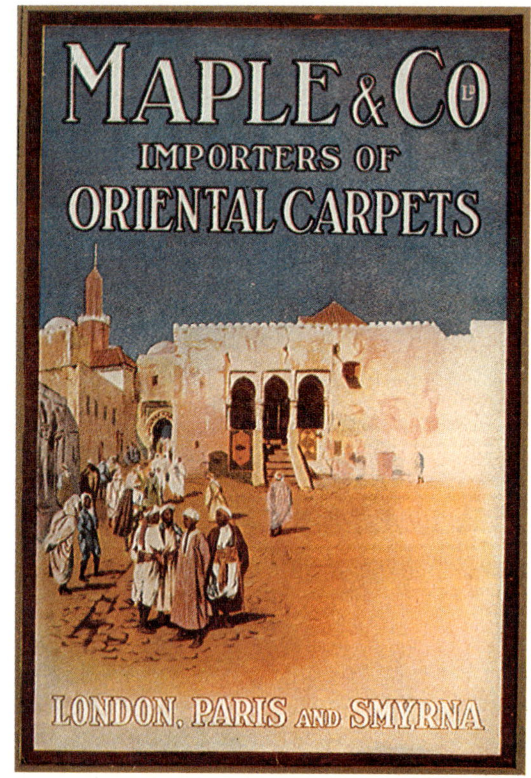

Illustration from J. A. Jordan & Son of Bilston, catalogue c.1928

"Black Cat"
Pure Matured
Virginia Cigarettes
HUNTLEY & PALMERS
GINGER NUTS
GUINNESS
IS GOOD
FOR YOU
GIVES YOU STRENGTH
BOVRIL
Makes
Contented
Cooks
SPECIAL
CIGARETTE
ELLIMAN'S
Sunlight
soap
VANTAS
ROYAL
WATSON'S
MATCHLESS CLEANSER
SOAP
Badge

Collectors

On the following pages we introduce ourselves and some of the other major contributors of original material for the colour section of this book.

Christopher Baglee & Andrew Morley

CB and AM were pioneers of enamel sign collecting in the 1960s, and through their Exhibition and book *Street Jewellery* have since established the collecting of enamel advertising signs as an accepted form of specialist collecting, joining the ranks of those other recently established collectables such as bottles, motorabilia, tins and cigarette packets.

Christopher and Andrew joined forces in 1975, and their comprehensive collection soon became well known throughout the North of England, so that by 1977 they were asked to mount an Exhibition of 150 of their best enamel advertising signs with loans from other private collections. This was first displayed in Newcastle upon Tyne in April 1978 and due to its instant success grew into a national touring exhibition visiting 18 major cities around Great Britain until June 1980. The catalogue produced for this exhibition formed the basis for the first book on the subject of enamel signs, called *Street Jewellery*. This book and the exhibition has firmly established Christopher and Andrew as leading authorities on the collecting and history of enamel signs. In this capacity they write regular features for national periodicals and continue to collect material and information, and to research the subject for publication. Their signs form the most comprehensive private collection in Great Britain, encompassing both the most familiar and the rarest types, examples of the latter appearing in this volume. Their collection, now referred to as Street Jewellery, is on permanent public display in the Linden Pub in the grounds of Linden Hall Hotel, Longhorsley, Northumberland.

The Authors

Street Jewellery Exhibition Mappin Art Gallery, Sheffield, June 1978

Part of the Baglee/Morley collection of Street Jewellery on permanent display at the Linden Hall Hotel, Northumberland

Liz Farrow

Liz Farrow, co-founder of 'Dodo Old Advertising' with Robin Farrow in 1960, has always been in the forefront of retailing all forms of early advertising art and display material. She began buying and selling such material in the late 1950s on the Portobello Road. Today, 'Dodo Old Advertising' in Westbourne Grove, London, is a delightful emporium for the most stylish examples of vintage advertising items including tin and paper packaging, enamel, card and glass adverts. Liz has always been keen to help other collectors find specific items for their own collections and indeed has in some way enhanced every other collection mentioned in this book.

Enamels were not always in demand; until about 1965 her basement was decorated with a fabulous patchwork of signs, which nobody wanted to buy. Then with the Carnaby Street 'fashionable nostalgia' boom, people began to take interest, and she has been selling them steadily ever since.

Those enamel signs that Liz has kept for her own pleasure include mainly those with interesting graphics and colour, and signs having both amusing and appealing illustrations. Her shop is still the main centre for vintage advertising, with its disarming sales slogan 'Dodo – purveyors of Junk'.

Liz Farrow in front of her shop Dodo Old Advertising

Christopher Gordon

Christopher Gordon

Christopher is also one of that small band who, whilst attending art school, started collecting memorabilia in the swinging '60s and thus now boasts an excellent, wide ranging selection of pictorial enamel advertising signs. He, like David Griffith, is now established as a recognised dealer in all advertising items relating to Victorian and Edwardian shops, including mirrors, tins, showcards, fixtures and fittings. He surrounds himself with a staggering array of vintage advertising material for both decoration and use, and this passion has even spread to include many items of automobilia.

David Griffith and Josephine Wright

David Griffith

David first became interested in early advertising material in the late 1960s, his original enthusiasm being for tins, (he is author of *Decorative Printed Tins*, Studio Vista) which soon widened to include all forms of display material. This early interest has eventually lead to him becoming established as one of the leading dealers in rare vintage advertising, which has enabled him to be selective in the choice of enamel signs that he and Josephine Wright have kept for their collection. Comprising some forty pictorial signs, this is by no means the largest collection, but David claims that the superior condition makes this the finest.

Robert Opie

Robert Opie

Robert's collection of packaging and sales promotion items is the largest and most comprehensive in the country, consisting of over 100,000 specimens, including posters, show cards, postcards, leaflets, manufacturer's free gifts, and, of course, about 100 enamel signs, many of which illustrate packaging, as can be seen in the photographs. Following the success of his influential exhibition at the Victoria & Albert Museum, called the 'Pack Age', he is now working on the establishment of a centre where the history of retail trading can be documented and studied.

Size: 17½"×11½". Date: 1910–1925
Collection: R. J. Hill

Original packages from Robert Opie's collection, showing products advertised by his enamel signs

Somerset Moore

Somerset has been collecting enamels since the early '70s and has done much to promote public interest in the subject by having them on permanent display in his fine seafood restaurant, The White Hart, Flitton, Bedfordshire. He has recently toured his collection around the south-east of England, to great popular acclaim.

Mike Standen

Mike is representative of the many collectors who are inspired by their professional involvement in advertising graphics. As a graphic designer himself, he has always been attracted to the unique visual qualities of enamels and has built up an excellent cross-section of the medium.

Barrie Pook

Barrie is an authority on motoring history especially as represented by printed material such as manufacturers' catalogues, posters, car manuals, specialist periodicals and advertising material (including give-aways and enamel signs). From his marvellous collection of motoring enamels, he has expanded his interest to include visually excellent enamels advertising other products.

Size: 22"×15"
Date: c.1930
Maker: Patent Enamel Co
Collection: Barrie Pook

Size: 36"×24"
Date: c.1930
Collection: Bluebell Railway

Size: 12"×18". Date: c.1910
Maker: Permanent Decorative Glass Co
Collection: Peter Birch

Size: 11"×9"
Date: 1930s
Collection: Baglee/Morley

Size: 27"×36"
Date: c.1905
Collection: Tom Richards

Size: 36"×24". Date: 1930s
Collection: Bill McAlpine

IPSWICH AND FELIXSTOWE
COCOA ESSENCE REGISTERED
Grate Polish
BRUNO
THE STANDARD DARK
FLAKE
Player's Please
FRY'S
CHOCOLATE
WESTWARD HO! SMOKING MIXTURE
THE SMOKER'S MATCH
SWAN VESTAS
WALNUT PLUG
CADBURY'S COCOA ESSENCE REGISTERED
FRY'S PURE BREAKFAST COCOA
VAN HOUTEN'S COCOA
QUAKER OATS
W.D.&H.O.WILLS
ZEBRA
BURMA SAUCE
TIZER
SHARP'S SUPER-KREEM TOFFEE
R.D.&J.B. FRASER LTD
FRASERS'
OGDEN'S
ST BRUNO
BOVRIL
Absolutely pure
4½D PER ¼LB TIN 4½D
Exhibition Gallery
STREET JEWELLERY
A HISTORY OF
ENAMEL ADVERTISING SIGNS
Christopher Baglee & Andrew Morley
New Cavendish Books
BROOKE BONDS TEA
COLMANS MUSTARD
PETTER OIL ENGINES
SWAN SOAP
PRATTS
PUCK
HUDSONS
PALETHORPES

In the wake of Street Jewellery

Since the exhibition and publication of our book *Street Jewellery*, the domestic consumer market, and the gift trade have produced many interesting products featuring enamel signs as their theme or basic design. Actual reproduction of original enamel advertising signs has been carried out by two companies: Relic Designs and Taddy's Tobacco Co. Ltd. Relic have produced a series of enamel back advertising chairs, including a copy of the classic Watson's Matchless Cleanser, plus a lovely example of an enamel boot black's stand, advertising Cherry Blossom boot polish. These items are part of a complete range of reproduction artifacts for use in the home, based mainly on Victorian shop fittings. Taddy's Tobacco Co. Ltd. is reviving all of the products of the original company which closed in the 1920s, ranging from the actual cigarettes in their original design packets, to various cigarette cards, and coupons for obtaining original enamel signs. This is a unique venture in product advertising revival, produced by and for the original and actual market. Along with Relic and Taddy's recent enamel reproductions, Dodo Designs continue to produce their successful range of enamel plaques, key rings, door plates, etc.

Other items incorporating enamel sign designs include the colourful sheets of wrapping paper and wall posters by Elgin Court Designs, a range of ready pasted vinyl wallpapers by Crown, a series of railway modellers miniature card versions of enamel signs by Tiny Signs, and a card index box produced by Ian Logan Associates. It seems that there is a wide application for the re-use of these old enamel designs in the modern nostalgia market, and we avidly await further developments.

Date: c.1900
Collection: Relic Designs

Original Chair
Collection: Baglee/Morley

Reproduction Chair, 1980
Reproduced by: Relic Designs

← *British and American editions of Street Jewellery and its Continental versions, a poster for the Street Jewellery exhibition, wallpaper by Crown and wrapping paper by Elgin Court Designs*

SMOKE
B.D.V.
TEA
THE WORLD
OXO
Blaydon Station

Bibliography

Automobilia, Michael Worthington-Williams, Batsford/RAC 1979

Bletchplakate, Axel Repenhausen, F. Coppenrath Verlag 1979

Cigarette Pack Art, Chris Mullen, Hamlyn 1979

Collecting for Tomorrow, Brian Jewell, Blandford Press 1979

Decorative Printed Tins, David Griffith, Studio Vista 1979

Emaille Borden, Jacques Stakenborg & Jaap van Zadelhoff Uitgeverij de Viergang 1979

Enamel Street Signs, Christopher Baglee & Andrew Morley, Everest House 1978

Geëmailleerde Reklame Plakkaten, Eigen Verleden & Tijd-Schrift 1979

Street Jewellery, Christopher Baglee & Andrew Morley, New Cavendish Books 1978

Periodicals

Everything Has A Value

Finders Keepers, monthly

The British Bottle Review, quarterly

The Cigarette Packet, quarterly

The Ephemerist, quarterly

ze: 36"×12"
te: 1920s
llection: David Stevens

Size: 30"×20"
Date: c.1920
Collection: Robert Opie

Size: 30"×50". Date: c.1925
Maker: WHS. Collection: Neville Summers

Museums & Public Displays

Since the publication of *Street Jewellery* in 1978 when we listed major museums and private railway lines displaying enamel signs, we feel that we should mention the following additions and omissions.

Bass Museum, Burton-on-Trent
Bourton-on-the-Water Motor Museum
Brewhouse Yard Museum, Nottingham
Kelham Island Industrial Museum, Sheffield
Linden Hall Hotel, Longhorsley, Northumberland
London Transport Museum, Covent Garden
Museum of Transport, Pollokshields, Glasgow
Madame Tussauds Chamber of Horrors, London
North Yorkshire Moors Railway
Ulster Folk & Transport Museum
Strathspey Railway, Aviemore

Size: 14"×18". Date: 1960s. Collection: Mick Forbes

Date: 1890s tray
Date: 1920s dish
Collection: Baglee/Morley

Date: 1920s
Bowl, collection: Baglee/Morley
Tray, collection: Graham Eastwood

Size: 18"×9"×10" approx. Date: c.1910
Maker: Falkirk Iron Co
Collection: Baglee/Morley

Date: c.1910
Collection: Paul Davies

Size: 8"×9"×12" approx
Date: c.1905

Porridge pan, collection: Baglee/Morley
Ash tray, collection: Leslie Longstaff

Index

Index of text references to signs, advertising companies, sign manufacturers and individuals, together with an index of signs illustrated in monochrome.

The Street Jewellery Society

Over the last five years the fraternity of enamel sign collectors has expanded greatly and the movement of information and signs through correspondence, magazine advertisements and through dealers has increased proportionally. Perhaps the time has come when machinery for the central processing of this information could be organised. We suggest that a Club or Society would fulfil this function and we would be pleased to offer the organisation for such a facility. If you would like to join such a Society and can provide stimulus and contributions towards it, then do contact us at 'The Street Jewellery Society', 48 St. George's Terrace, Jesmond, Newcastle upon Tyne, NE2 2SY.

CB & AM